KEYS TO FREEDOM

LEADER GUIDE

KEYS TO FREEDOM

LIVE FREE, STAY FREE

LEADER GUIDE

Keys to Freedom **Leader Guide by Mercy Multiplied Intl. Inc.**
Published by Mercy Multiplied
P.O. Box 111060
Nashville, TN 37222

www.mercymultiplied.com

Copyright © 2017 by Mercy Multiplied Intl, Revised 2021
All rights reserved

This book or parts thereof may not be reproduced in any form, stored in a retrieval system, or transmitted in any form by any means—electronic, mechanical, photocopy, recording, or otherwise—without prior written permission of the publisher, except as provided by United States of America copyright law.

Unless otherwise noted, all Scripture quotations are taken from The Holy Bible, *New International Version*®, *NIV*®. Copyright © 1973, 1978, 1984, 2011 by Biblica, Inc.® Used by permission. All rights reserved worldwide.

Cover design by Mercyuk.org
Interior design by Beth Shagene, Page-Turner Design LLC

Visit the author's website at ***www.MercyMultiplied.com***.

ISBN: 978-0-9986485-1-4

While the author has made every effort to provide accurate telephone numbers and Internet addresses at the time of publication, neither the publisher nor the author assumes any responsibility for errors or for changes that occur after publication.

Second edition

Printed in the USA

Contents

A Note to Leaders	7
Before You Start	9
Important Tips for Group Meetings	13
Keys to Freedom: *Group Expectations*	19
When Outside Help Is Needed	21
Group Meeting Schedule and Format	25

GROUP MEETINGS

Initial Meeting: *Introduction and Setting the Stage*	29
Group Meeting Outline │ 32	
***Keys to Freedom* Agreement**	35
Key 1: *Committing and Connecting to Christ*	37
Group Meeting Outline │ 39	
Key 2: *Renewing the Mind*	43
Group Meeting Outline │ 45	
Key 3: *Healing Life's Hurts*	49
Group Meeting Outline │ 51	
Key 4: *Choosing to Forgive*	55
Group Meeting Outline │ 57	
Key 5: *Breaking Generational Patterns*	61
Group Meeting Outline │ 63	
Key 6: *Using Your Authority in Christ*	67
Group Meeting Outline │ 69	
Key 7: *Maintaining Lifelong Freedom*	73
Group Meeting Outline │ 75	
Optional Celebration Night	79

A Note to Leaders

Dear *Keys to Freedom* Leader,

Thank you for your willingness to lead others through the *Keys to Freedom* study! Whether you will be facilitating one person through the study or an entire small group, my prayer is that you will get a front row seat in watching God "[bind] up the brokenhearted, [proclaim] freedom for the captives and [release] from darkness . . . the prisoners" (Isaiah 61:1).

You may feel a sense of nervousness or anxiety as you step forward to lead others, but I want to remind you that God doesn't call the equipped; He equips the called. If you look throughout Scripture, God continually uses imperfect and unqualified people to carry out His mission in the world. 2 Peter 1:3–4 says, "His divine power has given us everything we need," so it's not about how great and powerful we are; it's about how great and powerful Christ is!

As a leader, it will be important for you to stay open, prayerful, and flexible. Everyone walks the journey to freedom at their own pace, so be prayerful and attentive to your group's needs. You may need to spend an additional week on one of the tougher topics, or you may choose to go through the entire study in two-week intervals instead of one week at a time. You have the freedom to create a timeline that meets your group's needs for working through the study. Corresponding videos to set up your group discussion each week are available at **MercyMultiplied.com/KeysLeader**.

Your role as Group Leader is to facilitate discussions with the group. You will not have all the answers to every question or have a solution to every problem and circumstance. Your role is to point them back to Jesus, *the* Freedom Giver! He is the only One who has the ability to heal broken hearts and set captives free. You cannot do for them what He *must* do for them as their Savior. The members in your group must decide if they want change or if they want to experience more of the same. The weight of change is on them, not on you, so do not let others hand you their responsibilities.

A Note to Leaders

Due to the nature of this study, it is possible that you will see and hear some difficult things from your group members. You may be tempted to wonder if someone's story or issues are too difficult for God. Let me just tell you that after ministering to young women since 1983, I am more convinced than ever that no matter what the problem is, Jesus Christ *is* the answer. Not only can He handle the worst and most difficult circumstances, but He can bring full healing and restoration. However, He uses His people—you and me—to point those who are struggling or hurting to Him, so I am thankful that you have answered the call to lead this study!

In the following pages of this Leader Guide, you will find everything you need to prepare, lead, and debrief your group meetings. Mercy wants to help equip you with all that you need to effectively lead others through this study. For that reason, we encourage churches, ministries, or organizations facilitating this study to offer a training session for all leaders that provides a general overview of the *Keys to Freedom* study, including vital training elements to make your leadership as effective as possible. I encourage you to make use of the informational and training videos that can be found at **MercyMultiplied.com/KeysLeader**. However, if you are leading this study outside of a church or organization, be sure that you fully review all the material in this Leader Guide and view the informational and training videos at **MercyMultiplied.com/KeysLeader**. I also encourage you to consider additional training through Mercy's MPower Workshops to help further equip you as you help and support others. For more information on the MPower Workshops, go to **MercyMultiplied.com/MPowerWorkshops**. For ongoing support and/or answers to questions that you might have regarding the study, feel free to contact our Outreach Team at outreach@mercymultiplied.com.

It is an honor to be on mission together with you for the kingdom!

Blessings,

Nancy Alcorn
Founder and President

Before You Start

Before facilitating a group or an individual through the *Keys to Freedom* study, please view the training and informational videos at **MercyMultiplied.com/KeysLeader** and thoroughly read through the pages of this Leader Guide. Consider each of the below suggestions before you start:

Be familiar with the study material.

- You cannot give away something that you don't carry! As such, we encourage you to first complete the *Keys to Freedom* study yourself before facilitating a group. You could do this as a participant in a study group or one-on-one with a Christian mentor or pastor. This will enable you to facilitate your group as someone who has personally studied, experienced, and applied the keys to freedom in your own life.

- We encourage you to personally complete the study again *each time* you facilitate it. This will keep the principles, scriptures, and key points fresh on your mind from week to week. It will also demonstrate to your group members that you are on this journey with them, and that you are facilitating the group as a fellow sojourner, not as someone who has already "arrived." We believe that God will continue to reveal and heal aspects of your life each time you complete the study!

Enlist others who can provide support.

- Have someone you can go to if you need prayer or additional help with anything that may come up in your group, such as a pastor in your church or a mentor of your own. You can seek out the additional support you need while keeping things as confidential as possible. Be prayerful about this individual as you write their name on the next page.

My Support Contact: _____

- Have a list available of trusted Christian counselors and/or Christian treatment programs in your area in case you need to refer a group participant(s) at any point during the study. We recommend checking local churches in your area that have counseling centers or an online referral source, such as ***aacc.net***.
- Enlist a team of at least two to three people to pray for you and your group through the duration of the study. You need to have a prayer covering over you personally and over your group. You may want to consider recruiting as many prayer partners as you have group participants to pray each week for a specific person in your group. Be prayerful about these individuals as you write their names below.

My Prayer Team

1. _____
2. _____
3. _____

NOTE: Do not share prayer requests that include confidential or sensitive information relating to participants without their permission.

Take care of you!

- As a facilitator, there may be times you feel you are giving out more than you are receiving back or feeling a little "dry." Be intentional about staying involved in your own local community of believers so they can pour into you as you pour into the people in your group. Stay committed to your own personal spiritual growth by having consistent time in the Word and in prayer. In John 15:1–17 we are encouraged to stay connected to the vine (Jesus) so that we can bear much fruit. As such, we have provided the following in this Leader Guide to encourage you in your personal connection to Christ:

- **Before each group meeting:**
  Take a few moments before each meeting to sit alone in God's presence and let Him fill your heart, mind, and spirit with His love and power, as well as to pray for your group time. There is space provided in the "*Before You Meet*" sections for you to reflect and journal during your prayer time.
- **After each group meeting:**
  It is important to take time to reflect on your group meetings each week and on how you are doing as a facilitator. Reflection questions are provided each week under the "*After You Meet*" section to prompt your reflection on the meeting and on your leadership while you pray and process anything needed with the Lord. Spend some time after each meeting to simply sit in His presence and let Him fill you with His love and strength after all that you have poured out to your group. Space is provided for you to journal and pray during your prayer time.

• Pray! Pray for the members of your group on a consistent basis. Pray that the Lord would open their hearts and minds and lead them to the places of healing and freedom that He has in His heart for them through this study!

Important Tips for Group Meetings

Below are suggested tips to make your group meetings as effective as possible. We strongly encourage you to do your best to follow these suggestions as we have found that they significantly impact the experience and effectiveness of a group.

Make your group a closed group.

The study is most effective if done in its entirety, from beginning to end, with the same group of people, so we suggest that you do not add new group members after the study has begun. In addition, due to the personal and potentially sensitive nature of the materials and questions in this study, your group members will likely develop rapport and trust with one another, and you do not want to disrupt that by bringing in new members.

Create a safe environment.

The success of your group will be based in part on how comfortable and safe everyone feels to share honestly within the discussions. Trust is an important aspect in making your group a place where real community can be formed; a place where individuals can be real and honest. The "Group Expectations" outline on page 19 shares principles to help you establish a safe environment. We encourage you to discuss these expectations with your group members during the first group meeting and continually throughout the study. You can download a copy of the "Group Expectations" at **Mercy Multiplied.com/KeysLeader** to print and pass out copies to each member.

We suggest that you do not get into the habit of "going around the circle" asking each person to contribute to the discussion as this can be stressful to some people who are reluctant to share. Continue to encourage those who are not contributing to the discussion by offering them an opportunity

to speak but refrain from making it appear obligatory. You can always connect with any individuals who did not contribute to the discussion after your meeting time to make sure they are still engaged in the study.

Begin and end each meeting with prayer.

It is the leading of the Holy Spirit within the study material that brings freedom into the lives of those in your group, so use this prayer time to acknowledge and point to the presence of God. It is important that everyone believe and trust that God is present and active in your time together and that His presence is vitally important.

Use the provided group meeting outlines as needed.

The outlines provided in this Leader Guide are designed to help prompt discussion during your group meetings. The questions are suggestions as a jumping-off point; you do not have to ask every single question. You will be prompted before each group meeting to thoroughly review the discussion questions and make note of the ones that you want to cover in your group time, as you may not have time to cover them all. The main goal is simply for your group to stay focused on discussing the freedom key they studied during the preceding week. Our prayer is that your group members will find great encouragement and experience freedom by sharing their stories with one another and connecting within the group.

Encourage discussion.

You want your group members to be highly engaged in discussing the material. Your role is to help conversation move, not to give everyone a lecture or all the answers. Redirect questions and dialogue back to the group whenever possible. If you have examples or a word of wisdom, be sure to share when the time is right as led by the Holy Spirit.

Tips for fostering good group discussion:

- Use silence as a powerful tool. Don't feel that you must fill every quiet moment with something. Let the Holy Spirit work!
- Ask questions that are open-ended and require more than a "yes" or "no" answer.
- If your question does not get an immediate response, don't feel that you must jump in and answer it yourself. Allow your group members time to process what has been asked.
- Don't be satisfied with the first response to a question. Prompt the group for several responses. This moves your group from merely answering the questions to engaging in a conversation. You may even want to occasionally question their responses to enable the group to dig deeper.
- If you are having a difficult time getting group members to share, consider breaking them up into groups of two or three and give them a question to discuss. Then ask a representative from each group to share some of the key ideas their group discussed.

NOTE: It is okay to laugh or cry with group members as they are sharing but remember to avoid physical touch while they are in the middle of sharing as it could distract or stop emotion. However, it is appropriate to hand a participant a tissue or offer an encouraging word and/or prayer after the group meeting to communicate support.

Be mindful of the room setup.

The physical setup of the room/group will influence the group discussion. A few things to consider:

- Make sure the room is arranged in a way that allows every group member to see everyone without obstacle. (Circles or squares are ideal.)
- If possible, make sure every group member is in a chair, and ask all group members to be sitting up (not lying on the ground or reclining on a couch).

- As the Group Leader, it is best for you to sit among the group instead of standing in front of them. This way the meeting doesn't have the feel of a classroom setting where everyone is listening to one person teach but instead sets the atmosphere for group discussion.
- There are corresponding introductory videos for each week of the study to watch together during the group meetings. To play a video during a meeting, you will need to be able to display the video from the internet on to a TV or computer that everyone is able to gather around to view.

Offer continual review.

This study introduces key principles of freedom to participants and is not a formula or "step-by-step" plan. Every life and situation is unique, and therefore the principles will work themselves out in different ways. Ask the group each week if anyone has experienced a breakthrough or important revelation in any of the previous weeks' keys to freedom. For example, forgiveness is covered in Week 4, but it may not be until Week 7 that someone experiences a revelation regarding the power of forgiveness at work in their life. You will want to create space for thoughts and feedback on any of the keys each time you meet with the group. Continually remind them that the journey to freedom is a process, not a one-time event.

Set boundaries and be timely.

Be intentional about beginning and ending your group meetings on time. You may remain for individual discussion after the meeting, but you will likely want to let your group know in advance that you will be able to stay only for a specific amount of time after each group meeting. This will help to prevent group participants from trying to use the post-meeting time for personal counseling.

Do not allow children into the group meetings.

The presence of a baby or children will greatly distract participants, and the issues being discussed may be inappropriate for children to overhear. Encourage your group members to find a babysitter, or you may consider having a childcare service for those in your group.

Encourage continual commitment from participants.

After sharing the "Group Expectations" in your first meeting, encourage group members in their agreement with these values and commitment to complete the study all the way through. If it appears that an individual is no longer committed to the study or has been violating any of the "Group Expectations" outlined in the guide, consider speaking with them one-on-one to discuss the issue(s). Extend truth, grace, and prayer as the Holy Spirit leads you in this conversation. In extreme circumstances, you may need to decide whether they should continue attending the group meetings. Let them know that if they choose to discontinue now but desire to rejoin the study at a later time, you may be able to connect them with another group or with a mature Christian who will lead them through the study one-on-one.

KEYS TO FREEDOM
Group Expectations

The following principles help to provide a safe and nurturing environment for groups going through the *Keys to Freedom* study. As a participant it will be beneficial to regularly review and commit to these expectations throughout your time in the study.

What this group is and is NOT:

This group is intended for individuals who are ready to navigate their lives into a greater place of freedom, wholeness, and understanding using Biblical principles of transformation. This is not a mental health support group or self-help group. This is not a place where you will find professional help, and your Group Leader is likely not a licensed counselor or psychologist. Therefore, you should not expect that your personal issues will be discussed extensively during group meetings. Your Group Leader will make referrals and recommendations if a group member needs further help or support.

Group Values

Involvement

We want every participant to feel like a valued member of the group and we want to avoid turning discussion time into a one-on-one dialogue that everyone else just observes. The Group Leader will encourage participants who tend to monopolize the group time to allow other group members the opportunity to share. Honest questions from participants are encouraged, but the Group Leader may not always be able to address them during the group time. If this happens, the Group Leader will address the question outside of the group meeting.

Honesty

Sharing with honesty and authenticity demonstrates our genuine desire to grow and find freedom in Christ without hiding behind masks. However, we want to establish a culture where sharing is done with wisdom so that there is not a sense of people "competing," or even taking pride in their struggles. We will maintain a healthy balance between sharing honestly while not celebrating or glorifying our past behaviors and/or current struggles.

Confidentiality and Trust

It is important that everyone in this group make a strong commitment to one another to not discuss anything shared inside of the group time when outside the group. The exception to this rule is if you are threatening to harm yourself or others or if you disclose that you know of a minor being abused. In this case, the Group Leader is legally required to report this information to an outside source.

Respect

Fostering respect in this group is a key ingredient to this group's success. Disrespect will not be allowed. People can and will disagree about ideas and opinions, but you must not attack the worth of another participant or their viewpoint. All of us must listen to one another as we seek to understand and grow alongside one another. We must not negatively accuse one another, no matter how unusual opinions that are shared may be.

Commitment and Participation

It is expected that all group members will complete the week's homework before coming to the group meeting and commit to attend meetings. It is also expected that all group members will be involved in group meetings by thinking, feeling, and making decisions about what is being discussed, whether or not you share verbally.

When Outside Help Is Needed

The *Keys to Freedom* study will help individuals who want to go deeper in their faith and encounter new levels of freedom. However, there may be times when you have someone in your group who is dealing with serious psychological issues and/or heavy hurts. In those situations, you should consider referring the individual to someone who has more expertise, such as a counselor. If that happens, don't be discouraged. Making a referral is not failure or falling short!

If you believe a participant needs outside help, communicate your love and care for the individual one-on-one, but clearly communicate that you believe he or she needs help from someone with more expertise. Assure the individual that you will still be there for him or her, and this does not mean that your relationship will end.

Conversations like this will always require healthy boundaries to help bring a dividing line between your responsibilities as a facilitator and the responsibility of the participant. As a facilitator, your responsibilities are to communicate your concerns with compassion, offer an appropriate referral or "next step," and to ensure your own health and wellbeing throughout this process by working with other people and/or professionals to support group participants when necessary.

The participant's wellbeing is ultimately the participant's responsibility, and it is their right to turn down any support offered. If a participant becomes disruptive within the group and continues to refuse additional support, firm boundaries may be required to bring resolution. This may include asking the participant to no longer be part of the current group but to consider future groups after resolving the challenging behaviors.

When to Enlist Help

- When the situation involves any violation of the law
- When there is a mental health/psychological concern of any kind
- When any kind of alleged abuse is shared (NOTE: You are required by law to report any form of alleged child abuse. See instructions below.)
- When there is talk of suicidal ideation
- When you feel like you are "in over your head"

If Someone Is Threatening to Harm Someone Else

A criminal threat involves one person threatening someone else with physical harm. The threat must be communicated in some way, though it does not necessarily have to be verbal. You should contact local authorities if someone in your group mentions thoughts or plans to harm another person.

Reporting Suspected Child Abuse

Anyone can report suspected child abuse and/or neglect. Reporting alleged abuse and/or neglect can protect a child and get help for a family. It may even save a child's life. In many states, any person who suspects child abuse and/or neglect is required by law to report it. If you suspect that a minor who is connected to your group in any way is being abused and/or neglected, contact your local Child Protective Services office or law enforcement agency so professionals can assess the situation. Many states have a toll-free number to call to report suspected child abuse and/or neglect. To find out where to call, visit nccafv.org/child_abuse_reporting_numbers_co.htm.

Confidentiality and Sensitivity

If someone wants to tell you or the group something "as long as you promise not to tell anyone," let the individual know that while the group has committed to keeping group discussion confidential, you as the Group Leader cannot make that promise without knowing what will be shared. However, you can promise to do what you believe is best with the information they share. You can also promise that you will not take information that they share outside of the group without involving them and/or fully informing them first.

Group Meeting Schedule

While you have the freedom to create a timeline of the study that meets your group's needs, below is a proposed schedule for groups moving through the study on a weekly basis:

Week 1: **INTRODUCTION AND SETTING THE STAGE**

Week 2: **KEY 1**—*Committing and Connecting to Christ*

Week 3: **KEY 2**—*Renewing the Mind*

Week 4: **KEY 3**—*Healing Life's Hurts*

Week 5: **KEY 4**—*Choosing to Forgive*

Week 6: **KEY 5**—*Breaking Generational Patterns*

Week 7: **KEY 6**—*Using Your Authority in Christ*

Week 8: **KEY 7**—*Maintaining Lifelong Freedom*

Optional Week 9: **CELEBRATION NIGHT**

Group Meeting Format

Listed below are suggested approximate timeframes for each proposed element of group meetings:

Initial Group Meeting:

- **30 MIN:** Welcome, Prayer, and Introductions
- **5 MIN:** Video
- **20–30 MIN:** Discussion Questions
- **10 MIN:** Wrap-Up and Prayer

All Subsequent Group Meetings:

- **10 MIN:** Transition and Catch-up
- **10 MIN:** Prayer and Introduction
- **5 MIN:** Video
- **30–40 MIN:** Discussion Questions
- **10 MIN:** Wrap-Up and Prayer

GROUP MEETINGS

Initial Meeting
Introduction and Setting the Stage

Overview

Setting the Stage outlines the relationship between behaviors, beliefs, and backgrounds, and participants will be prompted to identify roots and behaviors in their own life. As a result of the tree analogy (discussed on pages 15–18 in the *Keys to Freedom* study) highlighting areas of their lives to which God wants to bring healing, participants will be growing in their own self-awareness. They will also be empowered this week to recognize the voice of God for themselves. Some may recognize the voice of God for the very first time, while others may be fine-tuning their awareness of how God speaks to them. Participants may experience a range of emotions as they begin to realize that healing is available to them.

Before You Meet

Give copies of *Keys to Freedom* to your group members prior to the first group meeting and ask them to read and work through "About this Study," "Introduction," and "Setting the Stage" (see pages 11–28 in the *Keys to Freedom* study) *before* your first meeting.

Download and print copies of the "*Keys to Freedom* Agreement" to pass out to each of your group members at your first meeting. You can find a downloadable PDF of this agreement at **MercyMultiplied.com/KeysLeader**.

Thoroughly review this week's "Group Meeting Outline" in preparation for the meeting. Refer to "Important Tips for Group Meetings" to help you plan for an effective time together. Ensure your meeting room is set up for the group and materials are ready.

Initial Meeting: *Introduction and Setting the Stage*

Thinking back to your experience as a participant in the *Key to Freedom* study, what were some of the most helpful things you gained? How did your personal relationship with the Lord change or grow during that time?

What led you to the decision to facilitate this *Keys to Freedom* group?

What are you most excited about? What are some of your goals for your group?

Do you have any fears or concerns about facilitating this study? If so, use the space below to pray through and process those things with the Lord. Ask Him for His perspective on your concerns. Write what He shows you below.

 **Initial Meeting:** *Introduction and Setting the Stage*

Spend some time in God's presence as you prepare for this week's group meeting. Reflect on the following:

- Ask the Lord what is on His heart for you personally, your group members, and your group meeting this week.
- Pray for the Lord to open the hearts and minds of your group members to receive all that He has in store for them through this week's study and group discussion. Pray that He would give each of them revelation on the root issues at work in their lives.
- Pray for any other burdens that might be heavy on your heart and mind today.

Initial Meeting: Introduction and Setting the Stage  KEYS TO FREEDOM

Introduction and Setting the Stage
Group Meeting Outline

Welcome and Introduction

1. Welcome everyone and begin the meeting by leading the group in prayer.
2. Share a little about yourself so participants can get to know you as the Group Leader. You can share about your family, job, what led you to facilitate the study, etc.
3. Go around the room and ask everyone to share a little about themselves (family, job, etc) and what drew them to the study. Encourage participants to keep their sharing to 1–2 minutes per person.
4. Communicate the scheduled dates/times for all group meetings (see page 25 for recommendations).
5. Review the "Group Expectations" (see pages 19–20). It is important to discuss these expectations very clearly as your first meeting will set the tone for the rest of your time together.
6. Hand out and review the "*Keys to Freedom* Agreement" (see page 35). Ask group members to sign the agreement as their sincere commitment to complete the study. They do not need to turn this in but may choose to keep it in their *Keys to Freedom* study book or keep it somewhere visible in their home.

Video

Watch the "Setting the Stage" introductory video together.

Initial Meeting: *Introduction and Setting the Stage*

Discussion

1. Ask: ***How did your first week of study go? What was it like to begin this study? Was it challenging? Exciting? Scary?*** Ask participants to choose 2–3 words to describe their first week.
2. Go through the past week's study together and discuss any questions that are marked with the leaf graphic 🍃, along with any additional key concepts that you want the group to discuss together.

Wrap-Up

1. Share that the homework this week will be Key 1: "Committing and Connecting to Christ."
2. Ask everyone to think of one word that represents what they would like to receive from God through this study (e.g., healing, joy, peace, freedom, life). You could ask everyone to simply say their word out loud to start your closing prayer.
3. Close in prayer:

   Thank you, Father, that Your plans for us over the coming weeks are beyond what we could ask or imagine right now. Thank You that You have made it possible for us to live in complete freedom and wholeness! We pray for Your Holy Spirit to infuse each page and each group meeting with Your truth, healing, power, and revelation. Protect each of us from the plans and schemes of the enemy as we work through this study. Give us courage and wisdom to know how to practically apply each key to the rest of our lives. Thank You in advance for all that You are going to do as a result of us spending these next few weeks together. In Jesus' Name, Amen.

Initial Meeting: *Introduction and Setting the Stage*

After You Meet

Talk to the Lord and reflect on the group meeting—what went well and/or areas where the group may have struggled. Give Him time and space to give you His perspective and His guidance on any areas where you need direction.

Pray for your group members as they study Key 1: "Committing and Connecting to Christ" throughout this week. Pray for the Lord to open their hearts and minds to receive all that He has for them through this week's study. Pray that each group member will make the choice to fully commit and connect to Jesus. Pray for any individuals who shared prayer needs at the group meeting or who seem to be particularly struggling.

KEYS TO FREEDOM
Agreement*

Every life is unique; therefore, every person's pain and struggle is unique. I choose to accept that my issues and my pain cannot be compared to those of another.

I acknowledge that total commitment to the *Keys to Freedom* study is required to discover the healing and freedom that I desire. Therefore, I choose to commit to complete each week's study prior to the group meetings. I choose to make all group meetings a priority to attend. I choose to fully participate in group meetings, whether sharing aloud and/or participating mentally and emotionally.

I commit to being honest with myself and with my group, my Group Leader, and God. I accept that I have to be honest and authentic to be able to apply God's truth that will set me free.

I commit to uphold confidentiality and respect of other group members. I will not repeat anything I hear about someone else's life.

I commit to not give any judgment, criticism, or evaluation of another participant. Each participant should be able to communicate his or her own thoughts and feelings without interruption or judgment.

I choose to be expectant for what God desires to do in me during this study, and I commit to approach my time with Him with an open heart.

SIGNATURE _____ DATE _____

*Copy and distribute to group members

Key 1

Committing and Connecting to Christ

Overview

Committing and Connecting to Christ identifies the importance of our relationship with Christ. Participants will be equipped to evaluate their connection with God and empowered to identify any false "stabilizers" in their life that have prevented them from committing fully to Christ. One of the most evident outcomes of connecting with Christ is a sense of renewed joy of the salvation experience. However, over-familiarity can often stand in the way of us receiving fresh insight and joy because we already think we have it. The questions in the homework for Key 1 will prompt participants to revisit their salvation moment and reflect on why they committed their lives to Jesus, including what life was like before Him.

Before You Meet

Thoroughly review this week's "Group Meeting Outline" in preparation for the meeting.

In the homework for Key 2, participants will be asked to make truth statement cards. Consider providing index cards (approximately 6 per person) to hand out at the end of this week's group meeting in preparation for the Key 2 homework.

Key 1: *Committing and Connecting to Christ*

How has your personal commitment and connection to Christ impacted your own journey to freedom?

Spend some time in God's presence as you prepare for this week's group meeting. Reflect on the following:

- Ask the Lord what is on His heart for you personally, your group members, and your group meeting this week.
- Pray for the Lord to open the hearts and minds of your group members to receive all that He has for them through this week's study and group discussion.
- Pray for any other burdens that might be heavy on your heart and mind today.

Key 1: *Committing and Connecting to Christ*

Group Meeting Outline

Welcome and Introduction

Greet everyone and open your group time with prayer.

Video

Watch the "Committing and Connecting to Christ" introductory video together.

Discussion

1. To connect the group to the content of this week's discussion, briefly share your personal story of how you came to commit your life to Christ (2–3 minutes).

2. Ask: **Does anyone want to share a testimony of what you have experienced from the Lord this last week?** (Ask 2–3 participants to share, depending on time.)

3. Ask: **Did anyone decide this week to commit your life to Christ for the first time? If so, let's celebrate! Will you share what brought you to that place of commitment?**

4. Go through the past week's study together and discuss any questions that are marked with the leaf graphic 🍃, along with any additional key concepts that you want the group to discuss together.

Key 1: *Committing and Connecting to Christ*

Wrap-Up

1. Read this week's "Commitment to Freedom" statement together (found on page 44 of the *Keys to Freedom* study):

    Transformation requires a total commitment and connection to Christ. I can't simply offer part of my heart and life to God and expect to walk in freedom.

2. Explain to the group that their homework for the next group meeting will be Key 2: "Renewing the Mind." (If you brought index cards for the group members' Key 2 homework, hand them out at this time.)

3. Close in prayer:

    Father, thank You for Jesus. Thank You that because of what He has done, we can know You and connect with You personally. We choose to be committed to You, and we know that through this commitment we are guarding our future freedom. Thank You for hope restored. Thank You that You are our friend, Jesus. With You, we will never be lonely again. Thank You that we never outgrow our need for You. You are a good, good Father. We submit our lives to You, Holy Spirit, all over again. In Jesus' Name, Amen.

 **Key 1:** *Committing and Connecting to Christ*

After You Meet

Talk to the Lord and reflect on the group meeting—what went well and/or areas where the group may have struggled. Give Him time and space to give you His perspective and His guidance on any areas where you need direction.

Pray for your group members as they study Key 2: "Renewing the Mind" throughout this week. Pray for the Lord to open their hearts and minds to receive all that He has for them through this week's study. Pray for the Lord to reveal to each group member the specific lies they have believed that have resulted in various areas of struggle in their lives. Pray for any individuals who shared prayer needs at the group meeting or who seem to be particularly struggling.

Did anyone in your group share a specific prayer need or area of struggle? If so, consider how you can encourage them at some point in this upcoming week, such as sending an encouraging word or scripture, calling them to pray for them, sending them a note in the mail, etc.

Key 1: *Committing and Connecting to Christ*

Key 2
Renewing the Mind

Overview

Renewing the Mind educates and equips participants to recognize faulty thinking by rejecting the lie and replacing it with biblical truth. As participants reflect on the belief system that upholds their issues and struggles, you should see a healthy activation of the Word of God as they receive Truth in their prayer times and learn how to make the Word of God personal to them and their journey. For some participants, taking hold of that underlying thought/lie that motivates certain behaviors can seem just beyond their reach. If you find that someone in your group is struggling with this concept, they might find it useful to carry a small notebook with them and reflect on the questions below as they try and identify underlying beliefs:

- **What was the situation I was just in?**
- **What were my immediate emotions?**
- **What were my immediate thoughts?**
- **What was my immediate response/behavior?**

As a facilitator, you can prayerfully guide a participant through reflecting on these experiences to help them identify any underlying beliefs.

Before You Meet

Thoroughly review this week's "Group Meeting Outline" in preparation for the meeting.

A day or two before the group meeting, send out a reminder to group members about bringing the scripture cards they made on days 4 and 5 of this week's study.

Key 2: *Renewing the Mind*

How has the process of renewing the mind impacted your own journey to freedom?

Spend some time in God's presence as you prepare for this week's group meeting. Reflect on the following:

- Ask the Lord what is on His heart for you personally, your group members, and your group meeting this week.
- Pray for the Lord to open the hearts and minds of your group members to receive all that He has for them through this week's study and group discussion.
- Pray for any other burdens that might be heavy on your heart and mind today.

Key 2: *Renewing the Mind*
Group Meeting Outline

Welcome and Introduction

Greet everyone and open your group time with prayer.

Video

Watch the "Renewing the Mind" introductory video together.

Discussion

1. Ask: **Does anyone want to share a testimony of what you have experienced from the Lord this last week?** (Ask 2–3 participants to share, depending on time.)
2. As a group, review the trail analogy and the concepts of neurological pathways and neuroplasticity discussed in the *Keys to Freedom* study on page 46.
3. Read Romans 12:2 together. Ask: **How does this scripture support the trail analogy and the neuroplasticity of our brains?**
4. Ask: **Why do you think it is so important for us to renew our minds on a regular/daily basis?**
5. Go through the past week's study together and discuss any questions that are marked with the leaf graphic 🍃, along with any additional key concepts that you want the group to discuss together.
6. Ask: **What are some of the personal revelations that you had through the truth card exercise? As you began to choose your thoughts and line them up with God's Word, what did you experience?**

Key 2: *Renewing the Mind*

Wrap-Up

1. Read this week's "Commitment to Freedom" statement together (found on page 58 of the *Keys to Freedom* study):

   Renewing my mind is an active, ongoing process that leads to greater freedom as I commit to replacing untrue thoughts with truth from God's Word.

2. Remind the group that renewing the mind is a continual process, so encourage them to continue exercising this key throughout the study.

3. Explain to the group that their homework for the next group meeting will be on Key 3: "Healing Life's Hurts."

4. Close in prayer:

   Lord, thank You for giving us free will and the power to choose. Help us daily to renew our minds to think like You think. We give You permission to continue to highlight any false beliefs we have about You, ourselves, and others. Continue to heal us from the inside out each week. We love You, Jesus. Amen.

 KEYS TO FREEDOM

Key 2: *Renewing the Mind*

After You Meet

Talk to the Lord and reflect on the group meeting—what went well and/or areas where the group may have struggled. Give Him time and space to give you His perspective and His guidance on any areas where you need direction.

Pray for your group members as they study Key 3: "Healing Life's Hurts" throughout this week. Pray for the Lord to open their hearts and minds to receive all that He has for them through this week's study. Pray for the Lord to reveal to each group member what specific hurt(s) have contributed to areas of struggle in their lives today. (This may be the deepest point of the study for many group members, so we encourage you to ask your prayer partners for additional prayer support this week.) Pray for any individuals who shared prayer needs at the group meeting or who seem to be particularly struggling.

Did anyone in your group share a specific prayer need or area of struggle? If so, consider how you can encourage them at some point in this upcoming week, such as sending an encouraging word or scripture, calling them to pray for them, sending them a note in the mail, etc.

Key 2: *Renewing the Mind*

Key 3
Healing Life's Hurts

Overview

Healing Life's Hurts educates participants in the lasting effects of experiences of life hurts. They will be equipped to identify hurts and emotions in their own life and feel empowered to receive healing, manage emotions, and find freedom to move forward. As participants seek God and surrender these often very personal experiences in their lives, a divine exchange may take place where participants will begin to encounter God's grace and healing. Participants will experience a shift of perspective in knowing where Jesus was during times of pain and hardship. Remember that this may be just the start of a much deeper healing journey for some participants.

Some participants may feel frustrated as they desperately want to experience healing but feel they are unable to engage with painful memories in a healthy way. This could be because the memory won't go away and is overwhelming them to the point of distress, or they cannot seem to access the memory as if it has been locked away. These types of obstacles are often indicators of a distressing or disturbing memory with which the participants may need additional support. In these cases, it is advisable to help the participant access additional support suited to their needs. It may even be beneficial for the participant to leave the group to focus more on their personal healing. Refer to "When Outside Help is Needed" (see page 21) for guidance.

Key 3: *Healing Life's Hurts*

Before You Meet

Thoroughly review this week's "Group Meeting Outline" in preparation for the meeting.

How has the process of healing life's hurts impacted your own journey to freedom?

Spend some time in God's presence as you prepare for this week's group meeting. Reflect on the following:

- **Ask the Lord what is on His heart for you personally, your group members, and your group meeting this week.**
- **Pray for the Lord to open the hearts and minds of your group members to receive all that He has for them through this week's study and group discussion.**
- **Pray for any other burdens that might be heavy on your heart and mind today.**

Key 3: *Healing Life's Hurts*

Group Meeting Outline

Welcome and Introduction

Greet everyone and open your group time in prayer.

Video

Watch the "Healing Life's Hurts" introductory video together.

Discussion

1. Ask: **Does anyone want to share a testimony of what you have experienced from the Lord this last week?** (Ask 2–3 participants to share, depending on time.)
2. Go through the past week's study together and discuss any questions that are marked with the leaf graphic 🍃, along with any additional key concepts that you want the group to discuss together.
3. Ask: **Is anyone willing to share what their experience of processing a life hurt with God was like? What benefits did you receive? What was difficult about the process? Did you receive any specific revelations from the Lord?**

   If group members are reluctant to share, ask:
   - *Would anyone be willing to share specifically what you heard from the Lord this week?*
   - *Did anyone identify a lie that you have believed as a result of a life hurt?*

Wrap-Up

1. Read this week's "Commitment to Freedom" statement together (found on page 70 of the *Keys to Freedom* study):

    When I acknowledge the hurts I have experienced and invite the Lord to give me His perspective, I allow God to heal me and bring new levels of freedom and peace.

2. Celebrate the courage of your group members for their work over the past week and any breakthroughs they may have personally experienced. Encourage the group to keep applying the keys they have learned so far as they continue to move forward.

3. Explain to the group that their homework for the next group meeting will be on Key 4: "Choosing to Forgive."

4. Close in prayer:

    Father, thank You for giving us a practical way to prayerfully process our life hurts with You. Thank You that You hear us as we pour out our hearts, pains, joys, disappointments, tears, and celebrations with You. Please teach us how to live free from the pain of our pasts and to walk in the joy of Your presence. Help us to lay down our burdens at Your feet and to grab on tightly to the promises of Your Word. Empower us to move forward into the good plans You have for our lives and enable each of us to confidently step into the unique destiny and calling You have for us. We love You, Lord. In Jesus' Name, Amen.

After You Meet

Talk to the Lord and reflect on the group meeting—what went well and/or areas where the group may have struggled. Give Him time and space to give you His perspective and His guidance on any areas where you need direction.

Pray for your group members as they study Key 4: "Choosing to Forgive" throughout this week. Pray for the Lord to open their hearts and minds to receive all that He has for them through this week's study. Pray for the Lord to provide each group member a revelation of anyone in their lives who they need to forgive and pray that they will make the choice to forgive. Pray for any individuals who shared prayer needs at the group meeting or who seem to be particularly struggling.

Did anyone in your group share a specific prayer need or area of struggle? If so, consider how you can encourage them at some point in this upcoming week, such as sending an encouraging word or scripture, calling them to pray for them, sending them a note in the mail, etc.

Key 4
Choosing to Forgive

Overview

Choosing to Forgive teaches the importance of forgiveness and the common obstacles in forgiveness. Participants will be equipped to recognize areas of unforgiveness and feel empowered to release forgiveness. For some participants, this can be difficult as they explore, challenge, and take risks to overcome myths surrounding forgiveness. For some, the breakthrough moment may come as they recognize lies they have believed about forgiveness, and they will be able to forgive as a result of the truth they have encountered. For others, the evidence of the power of forgiveness may come when they sense a "fine-tuning" in their ability to recognize not only the voice of God, but the presence of God too. Forgiveness draws us close to the heart of God as we choose to trust Him to bring healing, restoration, justice, and vindication into our lives.

Before You Meet

Thoroughly review this week's "Group Meeting Outline" in preparation for the meeting.

How has the process of choosing to forgive impacted your own journey to freedom?

Key 4: *Choosing to Forgive*

Spend some time in God's presence as you prepare for this week's group meeting. Reflect on the following:

- **Ask the Lord what is on His heart for you personally, your group members, and your group meeting this week.**
- **Pray for the Lord to open the hearts and minds of your group members to receive all that He has for them through this week's study and group discussion.**
- **Pray for any other burdens that might be heavy on your heart and mind today.**

Key 4: *Choosing to Forgive*
Group Meeting Outline

Welcome and Introduction

Greet everyone and open your group time in prayer.

Video

Watch the "Choosing to Forgive" introductory video together.

Discussion

1. Ask: **Does anyone want to share a testimony of what you have experienced from the Lord this last week?** (Ask 2–3 participants to share, depending on time.)

2. Ask: **Has anyone ever personally experienced unforgiveness having a significant effect on their inner peace or joy? If so, would you be willing to share?**

3. Ask: **What has your perception of forgiveness been in the past?**

   If the group is having a hard time responding to this question, prompt them with additional leading questions such as: **For example, have you ever viewed forgiveness as a cruel or unfair commandment that God requires of us or have you viewed forgiveness as a key that the Lord has given for our freedom?**

4. Go through the past week's study together and discuss any questions that are marked with the leaf graphic 🍃, along with any additional key concepts that you want the group to discuss together.

5. Ask: **On Day 5, you were asked to identify someone who hurt you and then were asked to process and pray a prayer of forgiveness for them. Is anyone willing to share anything about your experience as you did this exercise? Was it difficult? Did you receive any personal revelations from the Lord? How did you feel afterward?**

Key 4: *Choosing to Forgive*

Wrap-Up

1. Read this week's "Commitment to Freedom" statement together (found on page 84 of the *Keys to Freedom* study):

   Forgiveness is a vital key to living in freedom. It is a choice of obedience, not a feeling, but my feelings will follow when I make the sincere commitment to forgive.

2. Explain to the group that their homework for the next group meeting will be Key 5: "Breaking Generational Patterns."

3. Close in prayer:

   Father, thank You that we have the privilege to choose to forgive others despite our feelings. Help each of us to operate in Your wisdom from above which is first of all pure and then peaceable when we forgive. Enable us by Your Spirit to know what healthy forgiveness is and is not. By faith, we choose to repent and receive forgiveness for all our sins and shortcomings, Lord. Empower us by Your Spirit to choose righteousness, peace, and joy in the Holy Spirit daily. By faith, we choose to forgive ourselves and anyone near or far who has harmed us. Give us wisdom in how to navigate these relationships from this point forward, surround us with Godly counsel, enable us to walk out forgiveness by choosing to live by what Your Word says, and teach us how to pray for our enemies. In Jesus' Name, Amen.

After You Meet

Talk to the Lord and reflect on the group meeting—what went well and/or areas where the group may have struggled. Give Him time and space to give you His perspective and His guidance on any areas where you need direction.

Pray for your group members as they study Key 5: "Breaking Generational Patterns." Pray for the Lord to open their hearts and minds to receive all that He has for them through this week's study. Pray for the Lord to reveal to each group member any patterns that have been passed down through the generations that they need to break. Pray for any individuals who shared prayer needs at the group meeting or who seem to be particularly struggling.

Did anyone in your group share a specific prayer need or area of struggle? If so, consider how you can encourage them at some point in this upcoming week, such as sending an encouraging word or scripture, calling them to pray for them, sending them a note in the mail, etc.

Key 5
Breaking Generational Patterns

Overview

Breaking Generational Patterns supports participants in identifying positive and negative patterns of behavior. Participants will feel empowered to break negative patterns and receive their full inheritances as a child of God. A key anticipated outcome of this week's study is realizing what it means to share in a Godly inheritance because we are adopted into the family of God. Participants will begin to acknowledge both positive and negative generational patterns and identify themselves as co-heirs with Christ.

Before You Meet

How has the process of breaking generational patterns impacted your own journey to freedom?

Thoroughly review this week's "Group Meeting Outline" in preparation for the meeting.

Key 5: *Breaking Generational Patterns*

Spend some time in God's presence as you prepare for this week's group meeting. Reflect on the following:

- **Ask the Lord what is on His heart for you personally, your group members, and your group meeting this week.**
- **Pray for the Lord to open the hearts and minds of your group members to receive all that He has for them through this week's study and group discussion.**
- **Pray for any other burdens that might be heavy on your heart and mind today.**

Key 5: *Breaking Generational Patterns*
Group Meeting Outline

Welcome and Introduction

Greet everyone and open your group time in prayer.

Video

Watch the "Breaking Generational Patterns" introductory video together.

Discussion

1. Ask: **Does anyone want to share a testimony of what you have experienced from the Lord this last week?** (Ask 2–3 participants to share, depending on time.)

2. Ask: **This week we learned that we have a new bloodline because of Jesus, and this bloodline is what gives us the power to break negative generational patterns. Was this a new concept for anyone? Did anyone have questions about it?**

3. Go through the past week's study together and discuss any questions that are marked with the leaf graphic, along with any additional key concepts that you want the group to discuss together.

Key 5: *Breaking Generational Patterns*

Wrap-Up

1. Read this week's "Commitment to Freedom" statement together (found on page 97 of the *Keys to Freedom* study):

   Breaking generational patterns comes by identifying and taking authority over them based on my authority as a follower of Jesus.

2. Explain to the group that their homework for the next group meeting will be on Key 6: "Using Your Authority in Christ."

3. Close in prayer:

   Lord, thank You for giving us a new bloodline that is stronger and more powerful than our earthly bloodlines. We thank You for the good and positive patterns that our families have given to us, and we also thank You for bringing light to any patterns in our families for which you want us to stand in the gap to end. We ask for You to continue to show us the practical steps that You desire us to take as we put an end to any negative patterns and replace them with blessings. Thank You for empowering us to walk in love, freedom, and wholeness to leave as legacies for future generations and thank You for pouring out Your abundant blessings on our families. In Jesus' Name, Amen.

 **Key 5:** *Breaking Generational Patterns*

After You Meet

Talk to the Lord and reflect on the group meeting—what went well and/or areas where the group may have struggled. Give Him time and space to give you His perspective and His guidance on any areas where you need direction.

Pray for your group members as they study Key 6: "Using Your Authority in Christ." Pray for the Lord to open their hearts and minds to receive all that He has for them through this week's study. Pray for the Lord to show each group member how they can practically walk in their authority as His child and overcome any areas of pressure that they are experiencing in their lives. Pray for any individuals who shared prayer needs at the group meeting or who seem to be particularly struggling.

Did anyone in your group share a specific prayer need or area of struggle? If so, consider how you can encourage them at some point in this upcoming week, such as sending an encouraging word or scripture, calling them to pray for them, sending them a note in the mail, etc.

Key 5: *Breaking Generational Patterns*

Key 6
Using Your Authority in Christ

Overview

Using Your Authority in Christ teaches participants what it means to take responsibility for their lives, submit to God, and be empowered to declare His Truth and pray with authority. As participants begin to practice the tools in this week's material, they may also begin to see how they can defend the healing they have received through the Name of Jesus, through prayer and praise, and through the Word of God. Prior to starting the *Keys to Freedom* study, participants may have been pushing into God "for" their victory, but by this week participants will learn to have the sense that they are pushing into God "from" a place of victory.

Before You Meet

Thoroughly review this week's "Group Meeting Outline" in preparation for the meeting.

During the final week of study, group members are asked to study the importance of having vision for their lives. There is an optional homework assignment (details are at the end of this week's "Group Meeting Outline") where group members are encouraged to create a vision board. If your group chooses to complete this optional homework, consider having poster board available for each group member to take home at the end of this week's group meeting.

Key 6: *Using Your Authority in Christ*

How has the process of using your authority in Christ impacted your own journey to freedom?

Spend some time in God's presence as you prepare for this week's group meeting. Reflect on the following:

- **Ask the Lord what is on His heart for you personally, your group members, and your group meeting this week.**
- **Pray for the Lord to open the hearts and minds of your group members to receive all that He has for them through this week's study and group discussion.**
- **Pray for any other burdens that might be heavy on your heart and mind today.**

Key 6: *Using Your Authority in Christ*
Group Meeting Outline

Welcome and Introduction

Greet everyone and open your group time in prayer.

Video

Watch the "Using Your Authority in Christ" introductory video together.

Discussion

1. Ask: **Does anyone want to share a testimony of what you have experienced from the Lord this last week?** (Ask 2–3 participants to share, depending on time.)
2. Ask: **Was the teaching on authority in Christ a new concept for anyone? Did anyone learn something about your authority as a believer that you did not know prior to this week?**
3. Ask: **Does anyone have any questions or areas of confusion around the concept of authority in Christ?**
4. Go through the past week's study together and discuss any questions that are marked with the leaf graphic 🍃, along with any additional key concepts that you want the group to discuss together.

Wrap-Up

1. Read this week's "Commitment to Freedom" statement together (found on page 112 of the *Keys to Freedom* study):

   God has given me the right and responsibility to rise up in my authority as a believer as I submit to Him and close the door on choices that result in a loss of freedom.

2. Honor your group for their commitment to completing the study together, contributing to the discussions and their own daily readings. Celebrate how far they have come!

3. Explain to the group that their homework for the next group meeting will be on Key 7: "Maintaining Lifelong Freedom."

4. **OPTIONAL HOMEWORK ASSIGNMENT FOR KEY 7**: *Maintaining Lifelong Freedom* teaches participants about the importance of having vision for their life. Consider assigning your group members to create a vision board along with their Key 7 homework. If your group chooses to participate in this optional homework, explain to the group that they can take a piece of poster board to write on, glue photos, articles, quotes, etc., that speak to and inspire them in the pursuit of their dreams and God-given vision. Encourage the group to bring their vision boards to share in the next group meeting.

5. Close in prayer:

   Father, thank You that it is for freedom's sake that Christ set us free. Thank You that we are able to make our own choices and can choose to love You and live a life free from life-controlling sin and bondage. Thank You for giving us peace that is active and fights to maintain its ground. God, please help us this week as we continue to use our authority as believers and as we learn to live out all of these principles in our lives. We are so thankful for You and Your love, Lord. In Jesus' Name, Amen.

Key 6: *Using Your Authority in Christ*

After You Meet

Talk to the Lord and reflect on the group meeting—what went well and/or areas where the group may have struggled. Give Him time and space to give you His perspective and His guidance on any areas where you need direction.

Pray for your group members as they study Key 7: "Maintaining Lifelong Freedom." Pray for the Lord to open their hearts and minds to receive all that He has for them through this week's study. Pray for the Lord to reveal to each participant any practical actions they can implement in their lives to help them walk in daily freedom. Pray that He will open their eyes to the vision and purposes that He has uniquely planned for them. Pray for any individuals who shared prayer needs at the group meeting or who seem to be particularly struggling.

Did anyone in your group share a specific prayer need or area of struggle? If so, consider how you can encourage them at some point in this upcoming week, such as sending an encouraging word or scripture, calling them to pray for them, sending them a note in the mail, etc.

Key 6: *Using Your Authority in Christ*

Key 7
Maintaining Lifelong Freedom

Overview

Maintaining Lifelong Freedom reminds participants of the importance of using the keys to freedom as part of an ongoing lifestyle to live free and stay free. Participants are encouraged to identify how they wish to move forward in their purpose in life as a result of freedom they have obtained. They can begin planning for the hopes and dreams they have for their future. Some participants may find it useful to seek additional guidance through a life coach, mentor, or further education/training to help them achieve their personal goals.

One obstacle that some participants may encounter is the sense of returning to the beginning, or back to "square one." This can occur when an individual has identified additional areas of their life that need healing. The truth is that healing happens in layers, and as such, God often uses specific events at different times in our lives to bring deeper healing. This is not "square one;" but instead is the start of a new and deeper level of healing which leads to deeper roots in Christ.

Before You Meet

Thoroughly review this week's "Group Meeting Outline" in preparation for the meeting.

If your group has determined to not participate in the *Optional Celebration Night* (see page 79), consider preparing something special for your final group meeting to signify their journey, such as a group dinner or providing a keepsake or memento for each participant. Congratulate your group on their successes and celebrate all that God has done in your time together!

Key 7: *Maintaining Lifelong Freedom*

What are some practical steps you have incorporated into your daily life to help you continually walk in freedom?

Spend some time in God's presence as you prepare for the last group meeting. Reflect on the following:

- Ask the Lord what is on His heart for you personally, your group members, and your group meeting this week.
- Pray for the Lord to open the hearts and minds of your group members to receive all that He has for them through this week's study and group discussion.
- Pray for any other burdens that might be heavy on your heart and mind today.

Key 7: *Maintaining Lifelong Freedom*

Key 7: *Maintaining Lifelong Freedom*
Group Meeting Outline

Welcome and Introduction

Greet everyone and open your group time in prayer.

Video

Watch the "Maintaining Lifelong Freedom" introductory video together.

Discussion

1. Ask: **Does anyone want to share a testimony of what you have experienced from the Lord this last week?** (Ask 2–3 participants to share, depending on time.)
2. Go through the past week's study together and discuss any questions that are marked with the leaf graphic 🍃, along with any additional key concepts that you want the group to discuss together.

Wrap-Up

Congratulate the group for all their hard work and commitment during this study!

1. Read this week's "Commitment to Freedom" statement together (found on page 125 of the *Keys to Freedom* study):

    Walking in freedom for a lifetime is a process, and I commit to staying in prayer, staying in the Word, and staying in fellowship and accountability with other strong believers. I commit to pursuing the destiny and calling that God has on my life.

Key 7: *Maintaining Lifelong Freedom*

2. ***If you are choosing to do the Optional Celebration Night*** (see page 79), remind the group that they can bring family and close friends as guests to the meeting. Let them know that they should come prepared to share what God has done in their life through the study.

   If you are NOT doing the Optional Celebration Night, ask each group member to share how the group can specifically pray for them as they move forward on their journey. (1–2 minutes per person)

3. Remind the group that keys will only unlock doors when they are used, and the keys they've received from this study should be continually put into practice. Read the "Commitment to Freedom" (found on page 129 of the *Keys to Freedom* study) together and ask everyone to sign and date it. (You can download copies of the "Commitment to Freedom" at **MercyMultiplied.com/KeysToFreedom**.)

4. Close in prayer:

   Father, thank You for the ways You have moved in our lives over these past weeks. Thank You for the good work that You have started in each of our lives and for being faithful to complete that good work. As we finish this study together, we commit to taking the keys to freedom in our hands and using them on a daily basis. We anticipate that as we do our part to put these keys to work, You will continue to bring new levels of healing, revelation, and freedom! Thank You for the unique seeds of purpose and destiny that You have placed in each one of our lives. Thank You that no matter what we have experienced or walked through, it is never too late for You to restore life and health to those seeds. We ask for You to continue to breathe Your living breath onto the seeds in our lives, and continue to show us how to partner with You as we move forward in the purposes that You have for each of us. Father, thank You for making all things new! Thank You that our pasts are behind us and that beautiful and full destinies are ahead. In Jesus' Name, Amen.

After You Meet

Talk to the Lord about the overall experience of facilitating the *Keys to Freedom* group; what went well and areas where the group and/or you personally might have struggled. Give Him time and space to give you His perspective on how the study went and His heart toward you as the Group Leader.

Pray for your group members as they prepare to incorporate the keys to freedom in their everyday life. Pray against the attacks of the enemy as they go from this group study. Pray for the Lord to continue to heal them and reveal truth to them. Thank Him for His faithfulness to complete the good work He has started in each of their lives. Pray for any individuals who shared prayer needs at the group meeting or who seem to be particularly struggling.

Key 7: *Maintaining Lifelong Freedom*

Consider sending an email or note to each individual group member this week to thank them for being part of the study group. Encourage them in their pursuit of freedom and share ways that you have specifically seen the Lord work in their lives throughout the study. (If your group does the "Optional Celebration Night," consider handing notes to each group member at that session.)

Were there any group members that you believe may be qualified to facilitate a *Keys to Freedom* study in the future? If so, reach out to those individuals and encourage them to consider facilitating the study!

Optional Celebration Night

An optional ending to the *Keys to Freedom* study is to have a closing session of celebration, testimonies and reviewing and signing the "Commitment to Freedom" (found on page 129 of the *Keys to Freedom* study) with the group together. You can download a PDF of the "Commitment to Freedom" at **MercyMultiplied.com/KeysToFreedom**.

Tell your group members in advance that they can bring family and/or close friends as guests for this closing session. You may also consider providing refreshments or a meal, followed by the group sharing. Below is a suggested order of events:

1. As the Group Leader, begin your time in prayer by thanking God for all that He has done throughout your group's time together.

2. Ask group members to share with everyone what they have learned and/or what God has done in their life through the study.
   NOTE: Depending on how long you have planned for the session, you may decide to place a time limit on individual sharing time.

3. After a participant has finished sharing, take a couple of minutes to pray over that individual together.

4. After all group members have shared and have been prayed over, ask them to stand up and read the "Commitment to Freedom" aloud as a group and then sign it.

5. Consider giving a keepsake or memento, such as a bookmark or small jewelry, to each group member as a continual reminder of your time together and the keys to freedom to which they have committed their lives.

6. Close your time together with a prayer over the group as they go and continue to walk out the keys to freedom they have received through this study!

Notes

Made in the USA
Columbia, SC
02 February 2024